# —THE—
# CHRISTMAS
# 🌿 TREE 🌿

A HAPPY CHRISTMAS

Joyeux Noël!

# THE CHRISTMAS TREE

## The Heart of Traditional Yuletide

BARBARA SEGALL

CLARKSON POTTER/PUBLISHERS
NEW YORK

For Peter Way

Information regarding photographs appears on page 80

Published by Clarkson N. Potter, Inc.,
201 East 50th Street, New York, New York 10022.
Member of the Crown Publishing Group.

Published in Great Britain by Ebury Press in 1995

Manufactured by Tien Wah Press, Singapore

Designed by **Alison Shackleton**
Illustrations by **Benjamin Perkins**
Picture research by **Nadine Bazar**

ISBN 0-517-70193-6

# Contents

hristmas, whatever your religious sense of it is, and once you get beyond the rush of activity and frantic present-buying, is essentially about the survival of hope in a dark season.

The potent Christian symbol for it is the birth of a child, but the secular symbol is that forest survivor, the Christmas tree. It has made its way into our homes, in the last five centuries, bringing its past mythology along, mingling with Victorian Christmas traditions and renewing Christmas associations for succeeding generations in the modern world.

Fir trees, ivy and holly, the plants most associated with wintry Christmas festivities, surround me at home. The hazel, hawthorn, oak and wild plum that form the hedges are all deciduous plants that lose their leaves in winter. But proud all through the changing seasons are the evergreens that, here as elsewhere, in Northern Europe and North America, in the mid-winter, give us, as they did our pre-Christian ancestors, courage to hope and believe in a warmth beyond the season.

Many of the evergreens that make the framework around Holly Cottage are spruces, firs and pines, collectively known as conifers, and from their ranks come the trees that are now grown commercially for Christmas.

Conifers are among the oldest plants in the world, dating from the Devonian period, an incredible 405 million years

ago. At first glance, they are plain and uncompli-
cated trees, growing as tall and straight as they can
to find the light in a forest setting. Their leaves or
needles may not excite as much as the varied
foliage of deciduous trees, but a closer look
reveals a luxuriant range of greens, greys and
shimmering blues. New shoots make bright
green exclamation marks at the end of each
old branch tip in spring, and when the trees
are mature, after ten years or so, fir cones of
varying and fantastic shapes bear the many
seeds the plant needs to make sure it survives.

Holly Cottage's fir tree collection is my natural inheritance,
the result of previous occupiers planting out their Christmas
trees after the holidays. Reminders of joyful family feasts, they
have now reached 50 feet (15 metres) or more in height and
are, indeed, more forest than indoor trees.

As we trim the tree each year with pretty baubles brought
out of ancient boxes full of family memories, the tree, whatever
its size, becomes the centre of light, hope and beauty, bringing
with it an old-fashioned magic, welcome in changing times.

B.J.S.
Holly Cottage, December 1994

Norway Spruce - Picea abies

# ℭHE TREE IN LEGEND

*Our tree became the talking tree of the fairy tales; legends and stories nestled like birds in its branches. Grandmother said it reminded her of the Tree of Knowledge. We put sheets of cotton wool under it for a snow field and Jake's pocket-mirror for a frozen lake.*

MY ÀNTONIA
WILLA CATHER, 1876-1947

The tree – whether it be a fir, pine or spruce – is at the heart of today's modern Christmas celebrations and its arrival indoors for the twelve days of the festive season is an eagerly awaited and exciting event. At face value, it is simply a support for delicate ornaments, shiny tinsel and coloured ribbons. But, like most Christmas customs that we take for granted, it has many layers of personal meaning and nostalgic pleasure for each family member gathered around it.

For a young child, the glow of the first remembered Christmas tree is itself like the most beautiful of tree decorations. As the child grows, that memory coalesces with others to become an amalgam of childhood Christmas times. Shimmering and iridescent, the memory goes forward from

Christmas to Christmas until the child becomes an adult and more and more memory baubles are added to the collection in the mind, as new ways are found each year to create Christmas afresh with family and friends.

This is as far as most of us want to go in finding out about the tree. But if we wish to know more, we can discover hidden threads of the common history of the Europeans and North Americans, who have embraced the tree's annual use with such holiday fervour.

Peace on Earth,
Goodwill alway,
And a very Happy
Christmas Day.

Part of the story originates with our ancestors. Evergreens, such as holly, box, ivy, bay, laurel and the conifers, able to hold their shiny leaves or aromatic needles through the long and cold winter months, are and have been a source of fascination to us and to our pre-Christian ancestors. In many ancient myths and legends, the central power lies in a sacred tree. For example, oak, willow, ash and date palm are among the trees that hold a place in Homeric, Chinese, Scandinavian and Arabian myth and legend.

In the minds of our pagan predecessors, most plants and animals held magical and mystical powers and, in particular, those evergreen plants that survived the blasts of winter were

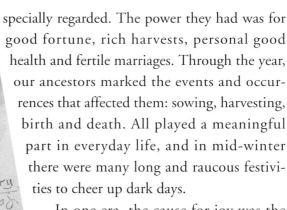

specially regarded. The power they had was for good fortune, rich harvests, personal good health and fertile marriages. Through the year, our ancestors marked the events and occurrences that affected them: sowing, harvesting, birth and death. All played a meaningful part in everyday life, and in mid-winter there were many long and raucous festivities to cheer up dark days.

In one era, the cause for joy was the birthday or awakening of the sun god, after the darkness preceeding the winter solstice in mid December. Later, our more settled ancestors found it was a good time to enjoy the feast of Saturn, the god of agriculture, celebrated in the second and third weeks of December. Homes and hearths were decorated with branches of these powerful evergreens, and feasting and jollity were the order of the day.

As December gave way to January, and the old year to the new, ancient Romans enjoyed a festival called the Kalends. It was a time when they gave each other gifts or *strenae*, usually holly itself, or other gifts accompanied with or decked with sprigs of evergreens.

Faced with people for whom the seasonal festivities marking sowing, growing, harvesting and feasting were of great significance, the elders of the early Christian Church realized they could not simply dismiss or ban these activities for their new converts. Instead, they adapted and crafted the festivals to fit with their own reasons for celebration. Our powerful evergreens kept their place at the feast but lost their power. They became mere ornaments and the power passed to the spirituality of the events surrounding the birth of Christ.

The early Church in Rome set the date for Christ's birthday in the middle of these pagan festivals. In Britain, ever

I wish you the happiest kind of Christmas ··

A MERRY CHRISTMAS
& HAPPY NEW YEAR.

since the Roman occupation (with the exception of Cromwell's Commonwealth, from 1649–60), the twelve days of Christmas, from 25 December to 6 January (the date of Christ's Epiphany), have been celebrated with varying degrees of enthusiasm.

Despite Christianity's adaptation and absorption of some of the feasts, symbols and customs of the pre-Christian past, the powerful evergreens were still a little too risky for the early church elders to cope with. In the year 575 church laws forbade the custom of garlanding houses with laurel and greenery, but their use continued quietly and secretively and resurfaced from time to time in written or spoken records.

Records from fifteenth-century writers in Italy and Germany note the use of hangings, flowers, branches and garlands of fir and other evergreens. As we know, trees other than evergreens also gave the Church cause for concern. Oaks, for example, were known to be powerful influences, especially for German druids.

The eighth-century English missionary, St Boniface, also known as Wynfrith of Crediton, took the gospel to these Germanic

*A Merry Christmas.*

druids. The story is told that one Christmas Eve he cut down a huge oak, used by the people he was working among as a sacrificial tree. In its place a young fir tree instantly sprang up. St Boniface and his newly converted Christian followers took it as a sign of the new faith. Perhaps this is the reason for the fir tree's Christmas traditions persisting so strongly in German folklore and legend, before spreading to other parts of Europe.

From a tenth-century Viking legend come references to the custom of celebrating Mother's Night, when the earth mother made visitations to her people. Descriptions of her clothes and jewels are elaborate and modern historians describe her as Mother Christmas. The tall, jewelled and decorated stick she carried is said to be symbolic of the sacred tree of pagan belief, and the origin of decorated Christmas trees in our homes.

Another twist in the story, also in the tenth century, is to be found in the writings of the Arabian geographer Georg Jakob who related what he called "eye-witness" accounts that embellished the importance of trees in the Christmas story. He told how, on the night of

Fröhliche Weihnachten.

Serie 200  No. 1398

Christ's birth, despite the wintry weather, all the forest trees flowered and fruited.

This magical moment was woven into the Coventry Mystery Play, *The Birth of Christ*, and is possibly behind the tale of the winter-flowering Glastonbury thorn, a hawthorn that flowers in mid-winter and is reputed to come from a tree planted by Joseph of Arimathea.

In Mystery Plays, the biblical dramas popular in England from the thirteenth to the sixteenth centuries, the Sacred or Paradise tree was used as a symbol of the Garden of Eden. This was usually a fir tree, and was hung with apples and surrounded by candles.

Mystery Plays were swept away, together with many so-called idolatrous aspects of the Church during the religious upheavals of the Reformation. Some commentators are adamant that the symbolic tree left the pageantry of the Church and was kept, clandestinely, perhaps, in the homes of the devout.

Still more legends come to greet the would-be Christmas-tree historian. From a German folk tale, the gift of winter

abundance comes in the shape of a forest tree. The story tells of a forester and his family in their poor home on a wild, cold night. Answering a knock at the door, the forester found a shivering child whom he brought indoors. The family fed him, gave him a warm place to sleep and, in the morning, they all woke to the sound of a choir. They realized their visitor was Christ himself and, as he left the cottage, he stripped a branch from a nearby tree, planted it in the ground and promised the forester and his family that it would always bring abundance in winter.

In 1516, on Epiphany (Twelfth Night), a descendant of the Paradise tree of the Mystery Plays made an appearance at the Christmas pageant given to the Court of Henry VIII. For William Dawson, a chronicler of Christmas in the late nineteenth century, it was a thread in the greater story of Christmas. In his wide-ranging work, *Christmas: its origin and associations, together with its historical events and festive celebrations during nineteen centuries*, he describes himself as a "snapper-up of everything relating to Christmastide". The "tree of gold" at Henry's pageant, hung with "roses and pomegranates", comes straight off the page and into our modern Christmas celebrations.

One sixteenth-century tradition links Martin Luther, the German leader of the Reformation, to the origins of the tree in the modern Christmas celebration. The story tells how, going home on a clear and starlit Christmas Eve, he set up a tree for his family, lighting it with numerous candles, mirroring his earlier joyful walk under a starry sky. Most historians of Christmas discount this as a fanciful story, but what is certain is

that Martin Luther, although an avid reformer, celebrated Christmas as a joyful, child-and-family-oriented festival.

Leaving legend aside, the first written evidence for a Christmas tree exists in the diaries and notes of a Strasburg resident of 1605, who noted that: "At Christmas they set up fir-trees in the parlours at Strasburg and hang thereon roses cut out of many-coloured papers, apples, wafers, gold-foil, sweets and so on." Strasburg was then part of Germany; today it is part of the French province of Alsace.

By the middle of the seventeenth century, other theologians of the Reformation, less tolerant than Luther, disapproved of the Christmas tree and its decorations as playthings for children. Despite such learned disapproval, the tradition of the tree flourished in German towns first, then gradually this practice spread into rural areas. More popular in Protestant homes, it later became accepted in Catholic homes as well, and its appearance inside churches began.

For a short while, in the mid seventeenth century, when Cromwell and his Puritan followers ruled England, all Christmas celebrations, garlands, greenery and decoration of any sort were banned by the Long Parliament in June 1647. Once the monarchy was reinstated in 1660, it took some years before the merry revelry formerly associated with Christmastime in England returned.

Given the strong Germanic traditions based on the Christmas tree in church commentaries and local legends, it seems natural that the tree tradition came to England from Germany. The first importers of the custom were German aristocracy, nobility and new members of the royal family, as well as German merchants who had established themselves in a number of English cities such as Manchester.

Princess Charlotte of Mecklenburg-Strelitz, who married King George III in 1761, was the first person in England known to have used the traditions of her childhood to entertain her own children. At successive Christmases she decorated small fir trees, lit with tapers and hung with presents of wax dolls, almonds and raisins.

Her niece, Princess Victoria, the future Queen of England, grew up with this tradition.

In her journal of 1833, Victoria, aged 14, refers to "two large round tables on which were placed trees hung with lights and sugar ornaments".

Outside the Court circle, the first mention of a Christmas tree in England came in 1789 in the diaries of Mrs Papendiek, when she records that her husband "proposed an illuminated tree according to the German tradition."

Although the tree was used by the royal family and by other aristocratic families in England, it wasn't well-known in ordinary homes. But in other parts of Europe the custom

spread quickly. By 1800 the use of Christmas trees in Finland was noted, and it was known in Denmark and Norway by 1830. Although it took many decades to become universally popular in these countries, many traditions quickly developed around the tree's use. In Norway, one such custom was for the family and friends all to join hands and circle the tree, singing, before they opened their presents.

The Christmas tree was introduced to France in 1840, when Princess Hélène of Mecklenburg brought a tree to Paris. By 1890 the popularity of the Christmas tree was such that between thirty and thirty-five thousand trees were sold in Parisian markets.

In England, the popularizing of the custom has always been attributed to Prince Albert, the German consort of Queen Victoria. In 1847, with five royal children to delight at Christmas, Albert wrote: "I must now seek in the children an echo of what Ernest [his brother] and I were in the old time, of what we felt and thought; and their delight in the Christmas-trees is not less than ours used to be."

After Albert's death in 1861, Queen Victoria lost her enthusiasm for Christmas, but the royal family's custom of decorating Christmas trees and giving presents was unstop-

La veillée de noël.

pable and had been widely adopted.

By the 1890s Christmas-tree markets in London's Covent Garden were well established. One retailer's records show that he could supply trees up to 40ft (12.2m) in height and that his sales topped thirty thousand trees every year.

In North America the tree entered the hearts and hearths of the nation much more swiftly after its arrival during the mid eighteenth century with Hessian mercenaries who came to fight in the War of Independence and settled, bringing with them many of their home customs. Within a few years they had established strong communities in various places. In the early part of the nineteenth century, there appeared in the diary of a Pennsylvanian settler, Mathew Zahm, the first written record of the later-to-become-familiar custom of a family going out to cut a Christmas tree. "Sally and our Thos. and Wm Hensel was out for Christmas trees on the hill at Kendricks Saw Mill," wrote Zahm on 20 December 1821. Written records like this map the spread of the Christmas tree through North America, from east to west.

The first trees used in North American homes were cut from natural forests or lumber plantations, but in 1851 the first commercial sale of trees took place in New York City. Mark Carr from the Catskill Mountains, north of New York, realized that there was a ready market in the city for mountain-cut trees. He took two sleds laden with trees into the city, and was soon sold out. He returned annually, and thirty years later there were over six hundred dealers selling trees imported from other parts of the country.

Similar tree markets existed throughout the country and, in New Jersey at the turn of the century, the first plantation was established with 25,000 Norway spruce. A few years later, customers could select and cut their own trees, a tradition which continues today on both sides of the Atlantic.

Whether the Christmas tree has its origins in the tree worship of our pre-Christian ancestors or in church customs, its place today as universal secular symbol of Christmas is assured.

Noble Fir - Abies procera

# TRIMMING AND LIGHTING THE TREE

*And now the fir tree...*
*    Acclaimed by eager, blue-eyed girls and boys,*
*Bursts into tinsel, fruit and glittering toys,*
*    And turns into a pyramid of light*

EUGENE LEE-HAMILTON
1845-1907

Christmas tree without any glittering ornaments would be a very dull affair. Decorating the tree is one of the season's great pleasures but how many of us stop to wonder how this custom began? Just as the Christmas tree's own complex history combines elements of pagan lore, Christian beliefs and modern commercialism, so does the story of the trimmings, decorations and lights that add sparkle and lustre to our holiday tree.

The pre-Christian practices of tree worship and reverence

for the natural world may not be readily acknowledged in a busy twentieth-century life, but some easily identifiable vestiges still exist.

For our ancestors, the autumn and winter loss of leaves in deciduous trees was a worrying event. It seemed to them that the spirit of the tree had deserted it. To lure the spirits back, they decorated or dressed the trees as attractively as they could. In many areas of Britain and

A Merry Christmas to you

northern Europe the practice of tree-dressing or decorating living, growing trees outdoors, was once a well-established custom. Today, in some communities, the ancient traditions of tree-dressing days have been revived by the British conservation charity Common Ground. Tree Dressing Day has been celebrated for a number of years in London and many other British cities and towns in early December by Common Ground supporters.

It is in Germany that most references to tree dressing are found. The Christianized pagans adopted the fir tree, which was symbolic of their conversion by St Boniface, and some commentaries say that they continued to decorate these trees outdoors. In the sixteenth century when the Mystery Plays fell from grace and the Paradise tree left the stage, many families brought a fir tree indoors in December to keep the faith they felt it symbolized alive in their homes.

The flowering and fruiting forest trees of Georg Jakob's tenth-century writings find an echo here too. In *Yule and Christmas* (1899), Alexander Tille, an historian of the German Christmas traditions, linked the custom of bringing bare branches of flowering plants indoors, to force them into

bloom, with the newer custom of decorating fir trees.

It is likely that candles came to the tree from the Erzebirge region of Germany, where, in the early 1700s, instead of a tree, a pyramid-shaped, wooden framework wrapped with greenery and decked with candles was used. These pyramids appear continuously in many European Christmas traditions. Whatever the origin of candles on the tree, light in this dark, winter season of the year was of great significance. In ancient times, fire and firelight were allied to the sun god and his worship. As time passed and Christianity took hold in much of Europe, illumination by sun, stars, candles and fire was linked to the power of Christ.

Once the practice of bringing small fir trees indoors became more popular, it was a short step from trimming trees outdoors to decorating them in the home. Wherever these early tree trimmings are recorded they are described as natural, home-made and usually very simple in style. Nuts, fruit, sweets, biscuits and bows of cloth, the easiest to hand, were the most likely choice for decorations.

By 1855, when the writings of Britain's Charles Dickens were well known on both sides of the Atlantic, decorations were not sophisticated, nor were they made on a commercial scale. Dickens wrote in an article for *Household Words* in 1854: "I have been looking on, this evening, at a merry company of children assembled around that pretty German toy, a Christmas tree. The tree was planted in the middle of a great round table, and towered high above their heads. It was brilliantly lighted by a multitude of little tapers; and everywhere sparkled and glittered with bright objects. There were rosy-cheeked dolls, hiding behind the green leaves; here were real watches dangling from innumerable twigs; there were jolly, broad-faced men – and no wonder, for their heads took off, and showed them to be full of sugar plums."

By 1856, when the first decorated tree was installed in the White House by President Franklin Pierce, the annual ritual of decorating a tree in the home to celebrate Christmas was spreading across America.

Like the tree itself, the first purpose-made, commercial tree trimmings came to Britain and America from Germany. Paper scraps, paste and dough shapes were the earliest types of decoration after the simple, edible and home-made variety of tree trims. As the popularity of the tree grew, the variety and intricacy of the ornaments available to decorate it also increased.

D'ACÍ·D'ALLÀ

Desembre
· de 1921 ·
· Número · de · Nadal ·

Paper, glass, metal, foil, papier-mâché plaster, cardboard, celluloid, plastic and even styrofoam are some of the materials that have been used by ornament-makers down the decades to furnish our trees with figures, fruits, stars and Santas, as well as fairies for the top of the tree.

Germany was the source of the first commercially made ornaments. One town in particular, Lauscha, in the Thuringian mountain area, then in the Saxe-Coburg-Gotha Empire, was the centre of this industry.

In 1867 when gas came to Lauscha, the glassblowers, whose industry was in decline, were able to use constantly hot yet adjustable gas flames. They began to experiment with the production of very delicate, thin glass shapes. They adapted and developed the glass ball ornaments or *kugeln* that many had previously used to decorate their own homes at the festive season. The earliest shapes were fruits, such as grapes, apples and pears, or were like pine cones, the fir tree's own decoration.

Emigrants from this area of Germany took their skills with them to North America in the 1840s and 1850s. In 1870, the technique of silvering the insides of the glass baubles to make them more reflective was improved and production increased.

In the 1890s the founder of the mass-market chain of stores, F. W. Woolworth, discovered the sales potential of these ornaments. He made annual buying trips to Lauscha and, in 1909, shop records show that he ordered 216,000 ornaments.

As the popularity of Santa Claus as the central figure in what was increasingly seen on both sides of the Atlantic as the commercialization of Christmas grew, so too did the tree-ornament industry. Candy-holders, shaped like cones or boxes, were followed by Santa shapes that came apart to reveal the sweets inside.

Such was the commercial appeal of Christmas that by the 1930s Santa himself metamorphosed from a slightly exotic

*Merry Christmas to you*

European figure, into a rosy-cheeked, chubby elderly man, epitomized in advertisements for the Coca-Cola Company by artist Haddon Sundblom.

The earliest trees used in homes were small, usually the tops of fir trees, or young trees measuring 3–4ft (90cm–1.2m). They could be placed in containers and weighted down to keep them steady and upright. But during the 1870s floor-to-ceiling-height trees, some up to 40ft (12.2m) tall, became popular.

With a greater expanse of tree to cover, the variety and range of tree trimmings available had to expand too. The choice in stores was wide and, in 1880, tinsel to garland the tree was on sale in many commercial outlets in North America.

Fashions in tree-trimming came and went. At first, trees were glittering and glowing confections, overflowing with gleaming, light-reflecting shapes, tinsel, baubles and figures. Then, at the turn of the nineteenth century, fashionable editors and writers advised that the overcrowded tree was

out and suggested that a "white tree" was more tasteful. Instead of the bright colours of earlier years, the white tree made its impact with shimmering silver tinsel, glass icicles, white candles and ornaments in silver or white.

Somehow, the "old-fashioned" tree, colourful and over-crowded, never quite disappeared and through the decades before the Second World War its ornaments continued to come from Germany, although by now Japanese manufacturers had also entered the market. However, in the 1940s, when America entered the war against Germany, imports from Germany were banned and American manufacturers began to support the continuing demand for ornaments. Among them

A HAPPY CHRISTMAS

was the Corning Glass Works of New York which in 1939 started to machine-produce two million ornaments a week.

In the 1950s, plastic, foil and styrofoam were the materials used for the mass-produced ornaments, but by the end of the decade German-made products were once again on offer in stores in Britain and North America.

From the middle of the 1970s the nostalgia for traditional Christmas celebrations grew, fuelling an interest in old decorations, and the blown-glass, moulded ornaments of the past are once again being created in Europe and America by skilled crafts people.

Today, ornaments, candy boxes and candle clips of the past, as well as fairly modern ones are highly collectable. In 1994, the auctioneers Christie's sold, among other Christmas objects, seventeen tinplate Christmas-tree candle-holders for £900.

New styles and shapes continue to be created, commissioned and sold in their millions to brighten the modern Christmas celebration. No doubt they will become the collectables of the future.

The most dangerous aspect of early tree-trimming was the use of candles to illuminate the already glistening, gleaming display. Early commentators advised that one member of the family should be detailed to become "fire-watcher" throughout the festivities. A heavy responsibility for such merry times. Others advised having a bucket filled with water at the ready and a damp sponge fixed to a long cane, to reach the top of the tree, should any of the upper branches catch fire.

At first, candles were simply fixed on to the tree with wire or string. Later, counter-balanced holders were developed, followed by clip-on candle holders. Lantern-like holders were part of the attempt to solve the problem. Beautiful as candle-light is, the safety aspects of candle power made it one of the more quickly replaced elements of decoration. Although traditionalists continued to insist that this was the only form of lighting fit for a Christmas tree, the invention of electric Christmas tree lights in the early 1880s provided the glow without fear of fire.

Electric tree lights were produced commercially in the 1890s, and were at

first expensive, retailing in North America at twelve dollars for 26 plain, frosted and red lamps. The styles of the bulbs or lamps varied from utilitarian to exotic. At first they were unreliable with rather basic wiring, and had to be handled carefully. If one bulb failed to work, none would work. Later developments included independently wired bulbs, whose individual failure didn't affect the working of the other lamps. Today, electric lights are relatively foolproof, but it is common to see people on Christmas Eve trying to buy replacements for bulbs that stopped working the previous Christmas and were put away, unchanged!

Early on in the story of trimming trees for Christmas, it became very obvious that for adults the greatest pleasure came from watching the delight in the eyes of children on first seeing the tree on Christmas Eve, trimmed and lit. As Santa Claus became the central figure at the party, children often thought it was Santa who decorated their trees, and in many homes, through the decades, parents went to enormous lengths and huge subterfuges to protect this fancy. Often they decorated

the trees themselves, behind closed doors, and only allowed the children in when everything was in place.

So it is today. Adults still find the greatest pleasure in the response of the young to the shimmer and shine of Christmas. Trimming the tree is as much part of the excitement and delight as ever it was. A London mother in the 1990s told how she enjoyed sharing the trimming of the tree with her two small daughters, appreciating their lop-sided but delightful efforts, and waiting until they had gone to bed before altering the arrangements to create a more aesthetically pleasing effect.

In times that are confusing and constantly in flux, there is something reassuring and joyful about such traditions continuing. That they do becomes obvious when you walk or drive along the streets or roads of any city, town, village or rural area in Europe or North America. You will find countless Christmas trees lit and trimmed, twinkling from many a window, offering a magical, memorable charm, just as their forerunners did centuries before in Germany.

Scots Pine - Pinus sylvestris

# ℙRESENTS UNDER THE TREE

*Today I have two children of my own to give presents to, who, they know not why, are full of happy wonder at the German Christmas tree and its radiant candles...*

PRINCE ALBERT IN A LETTER TO HIS FATHER
WINDSOR 1841

oday, the exchanging of presents at Christmas seems a natural part of the festivities, and it is difficult to imagine a tree with no colourfully wrapped and beribboned parcels beneath it.

The origins of giving gifts at this time of year lie far away in the precarious lives of our earliest farming ancestors, when the gifts were symbolic of survival and hope.

As hunting gave way to farming and manufacture, life became comparatively stable. Still, the winter was long, dark and, without the benefit of refrigeration and other modern means of making and preserving food, it was a time for careful use of precious resources. Once the mid-winter solstice was past, our ancestors knew that they were halfway through this dreary time.

Then gifts, usually of an edible nature, were given and our ancestors felt they could feast and enjoy some of the surplus of their store cupboards, sharing their largesse with friends, neighbours and family.

Roman gift-giving took place at their festival for the January Kalends. Their gifts or *strenae* still find an echo in the continuing French custom of New Year gifts called *étrennes*. At the heart of the Christian celebration is the gift of Jesus himself and New Year gifts became a commemoration of Epiphany. They echo the gifts of gold, frankincense and myrrh from the Magi. A modern form of church tree decoration, called

Chrismons (from Christian Monograms) uses many symbols including a seven-pointed star within a circle. This stands for the Ephipany star that guided the Magi and for the gift to the world of the Spirit.

Many of the early Christian saints are connected with gift-bearing to children. Indeed, St Nicholas, the fourth-century Bishop of Myra, whose feast day is 6 December, was renowned for his self-effacing acts of kindness to people from all walks of life, but especially to children.

With the changes brought about by the Reformation, it seems that the generosity of spirit St Nicholas was noted for was taken up by the subsequent gift-givers at the more secular feast that Christmas became. It can be detected in all the non-religious gift-bringers in many countries. Father Christmas, Papa Noël, Pelznickel and Santa Claus (brought to North America by Dutch immigrants as Sinter Klaas), owe their existence to St Nicholas.

However, up to the late sixteenth century, for the

devout it was still Christ who was seen as the central bringer of gifts at this season. Sermons of the time specifically referred to Christmas presents (directly translated as "Christ-bundles"). They included money, sugar-plums, cakes, apples, nuts, dolls; useful gifts such as clothes, as well as items that "belong to teaching, obedience, chastisement, and discipline, as A.B.C. tablets, Bibles and handsome books, writing materials, paper".

In France it was also the Christ Child who brought gifts, while in some parts of Italy it was a woman called Befana (her name is a corruption of the Italian word for Epiphany); in other parts, St Lucia carried the gifts. In Sweden, a secret gift-bearer delivered his or her presents swiftly and noisily. The gift was called a *Julklapp*, and was usually wrapped in many layers of paper to disguise its size.

The arrival of the decorated fir tree inside the house created a central place to either hold the presents or to have them nearby. In nineteenth-century Germany at these early celebrations around the tree, it seems that presents to delight or surprise were suspended from the tree itself, while any that were useful or practical found a place on a table near it.

Ever since St Francis of Assisi made the first Christmas crib in 1223, in many areas of Europe it has been customary to make and set up beautifully carved scenes of Christ's nativity. As the tree became the central focus of festivities in the home, these cribs were staged at the base of it. In many homes these cribs became part of the ritual of trimming the tree.

In the eighteenth and nineteenth centuries the custom was taken across the Atlantic to North America by successive waves of German emigrants, and was particularly popular with the Moravian settlers of Pennsylvania. In the twentieth century these crib scenes are not always individually hand-carved. Instead most are mass-made and the scope of some extends far beyond religious figures, to include music boxes playing carols, farmyards and village scenes to name but a few alternatives. Many of these variations to the "religious sets" were village building collections that could be lit up with small electric bulbs to lend, in the words of the Sears

'Mid
Plenty's cheer
A Happy Year!

Aunt Fischer.

Roebuck catalogue of 1931, "real Christmas atmosphere".

Cribs did not make a strong impact on secular English traditions until more recent times, but the practice of giving presents at Christmas did. In the early nineteenth century, Prince Albert and Queen Victoria set the trend for Christmas trees and many other related customs besides. Prior to this, the giving of gifts at New Year had been popular between adults, but it was not a universally adopted activity.

Prince Albert brought with him to England the German tradition of placing presents next to the tree. On Christmas Eve 1845, Queen Victoria noted in her journal: "At 6, Albert took me to the Blue Closet, where as usual my frosted tree

stood and my presents were all arranged on a table."

Christmas presents were given to the royal children, and Victoria and Albert gave gifts to all the members of their household. One of them, Eleanor Stanley, related how they all went "to the Oakroom, where the Queen and Prince already were, standing by a large table covered with a white cloth, in the middle of which was a little fir-tree. Round this were all our presents, with the name of each person written by the Queen on a slip of paper lying by the present." Although after Albert's death in 1861 Christmas for Victoria was never happy, the trend for present-giving was set.

From an article in *The Ladies' Treasury*, 1860, it was apparent that the custom of universal presents to all and sundry, as practised in Germany, as well as the substantial nature of some of the presents given, was not yet the popular vogue in England.

However, as the tree became more and more popular in England, it became the central feature at parties or gatherings for large groups of children. Among its decorations were "penny" toys or other trinkets described by Charles Dickens:

"there were fiddles and drums; there were tambourines, books, work-boxes, paint-boxes, sweetmeat-boxes, peep-show boxes, all kinds of boxes; there were trinkets for the elder girls ... there were baskets and pin-cushions in all devices; there were guns, swords and banners; there were witches standing in enchanted rings of paste-board."

These toys went on the tree unwrapped and were given to children during the festivities, often by lottery. This type of party, known simply as a "Christmas tree", was quite popular. A contributor to *The Ladies' Treasury* explained how to organize the distribution of presents, advising the host or hostess to "fasten a numbered ticket firmly on every gift, so that when a guest draws the corresponding ticket from a bag (to be carried round to the guests by the eldest daughter of the house), there may be no difficulty in assigning the prize."

The new life breathed into the English Christmas by the royal Victorians trickled down to reach all levels of society and the popularity of giving gifts heralded the birth of the most modern of Christmas customs, Christmas shopping.

Before 1870 the bulk of Christmas spending went on food and drink, but soon Father Christmas or Santa Claus made his appearance in advertisements, at parties and major stores. Children went with their parents to Christmas bazaars held in department stores. Ernest Shephard, illustrator of *Winnie the Pooh*, recalled one of his early visits to such a bazaar in the 1880s, where he saw Father Christmas, Punch and Judy and a "Bower of Dolls" presided over by an attractive fairy. For three-pence, children could dip into a bran tub and pull out a Christmas prize.

A few decades before, the idea of a present for everyone had seemed outlandish and foreign but, once retailers saw there was a new market to exploit, the custom of placing presents under the tree became firmly fixed as part of the festivities.

In the late twentieth century there is no looking back. In Europe, Christmas decorations and presents are on sale from October. In North America, the passing of Thanksgiving on 24 November ushers in the holiday season. However, really serious Christmas shoppers on both sides of the Atlantic are known to buy next year's presents immediately after Christmas in the January sales!

Colorado Blue Spruce - Picea pungens 'Glauca'

# Modern ALTERNATIVES

*So feast your eyes now*
  *On mimic star and moon-cold bauble:*
*Worlds may wither unseen*
  *But the Christmas Tree is a tree of fable,*
*A phoenix in evergreen,*
  *And the world cannot change or chill*
*what its mysteries mean*
  *To your hearts and eyes now*

THE CHRISTMAS TREE,
C. DAY LEWIS 1904-72

The charming tradition of having a decorated fir tree indoors has brought delight to revellers down the generations. However, it has not been without controversy. At almost the same moment that the general populace on both sides of the Atlantic adopted this custom, there came a wave of reaction against the idea of using a real tree.

In Germany there were trees aplenty, at first, for the relatively few who wished to bring them into their homes, and this was also the case in other parts of Europe and North America. But as the idea took hold, the feeling grew that for individuals to march into the forest to cut down what was the nation's resource was folly. Alternatives had to be found before the forests were denuded.

One of the first public figures to speak out against the practice was President Theodore Roosevelt, a noted conservationist.

Artificial trees entered the arena early. The Germans preferred small table-top trees, and these were in short supply. Many, especially those who emigrated to North America, took feather trees with them.

Another reason for preferring the artificial tree was because the trees that were

cut down by individuals or, later, entrepreneurs for selling off trucks at markets were often asymmetrical and lop-sided. They were quaint but not always attractive and certainly not easy to trim artistically.

A feather tree – sometimes called the Nuremberg Christmas tree – was the first purpose-made alternative. It came in several sizes, with the smallest, for use as a trim for presents, only two inches (5cm) tall. The next size up, for table-top use, was six inches (15cm) high, complete with holly berries at the end of each branch. Larger sizes were available, with 30in (75cm) a popular size.

The feathers, usually turkey or goose, but sometimes ostrich and swan, were dyed, the quills stripped off and then individually wired on to wooden branches. Feather trees were sparse-looking and absolutely symmetrical, mimicking the "ideal", perfect young fir tree.

Although the first purpose-grown Christmas trees were on sale in the early 1900s, there was still a market for artificial

trees, and feather trees continued to be imported from pre-
and post-war Germany.

Trees made in Japan were also sold in North America. As
ornaments became more sophisticated and electric light sets
cheaper and more reliable, the feather trees became more spec-
tacular. In 1929 the Sears Roebuck catalogue had an 8ft-high
tree (2.4m), with 96 main branches and 148 small branches. It
cost $8.98.

From the 1930s to 1960, new synthetic materials such as
cellophane, visca, plastic and green vinyl became available.
They were all put to use to simulate the real Christmas tree.

The first field-grown tree farm was planted in 1900 and

more reliably shaped real trees became available, but it was only in the 1970s that Christmas tree farmers pioneered new methods of growing trees that produced bushy but symmetrical shapes at sizes that most urban homes could accommodate. To achieve these shapes, the trees were machine-sheared annually as they grew in their regimented rows.

Although a natural peak – for a tree-top star or other decoration – was highly desirable, fashions in tree-trimming changed so radically by the middle of the twentieth century that the sparse look of the artificial and early live trees was no longer popular.

Needle-drop has often been a persuasive factor in the abandonment of real trees at Christmas and, in modern times, with the advent of central heating, trees tend to lose their needles even more quickly than their counterparts of a century ago.

Artificial trees today have to look like the real thing and provide all the nostalgia

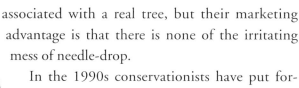

Glædelig Jul

associated with a real tree, but their marketing advantage is that there is none of the irritating mess of needle-drop.

In the 1990s conservationists have put forward the view that, although the initial outlay for a superb specimen of "Pinus plasticus" is high, it is relatively cheaper than buying a real tree. The artificial tree is safer to use and is maintenance-free.

Sparked off annually in newspapers and in homes, this real versus fake tree debate continues. Forestry departments and commercial Christmas-tree growers involved in a multi-million-pound worldwide industry, proclaim the ecologically sound nature of their business. Each tree converts 2.7lbs (1.2k) of carbon dioxide into carbon and oxygen each year, with the 40 million grown annually in Britain alone ridding us of 50,000 tons of carbon dioxide. They argue further that they plant two for every one tree harvested; they claim that the plantations under

cultivation are beneficial to the environment, benefit wildlife habitats, soil conservation and provide green spaces in areas of increasing urbanization. They are also quick to point out the waste of plastic, oils and other fuels in the production of the fake versions.

In Britain in 1994, offering a middle route through the debate, one tree farm advertised for sale 50,000 12in-high (30cm) potted trees for table-top use. After Christmas the trees could be planted out and grown on in the garden.

Make-your-own enthusiasts have a wide choice of garden material to choose from. Birch branches (favoured in Scandinavian countries), the coloured stems of cogwoods and even holly branches, bright with variegated foliage or shining with glossy berries, are suitable as alternatives for the holiday tree.

If make-your-own doesn't appeal, there is a wide range of mass-made twiggery-pokery offered in the stores. Trees made from coiled twigs, woven twigs and mossed wire and twig confections, in a variety of sizes, are just a few of the options.

Nordmann Fir – *Abies nordmanniana*

# Ⓨour own tree

*O Christmas Tree, O Christmas Tree,*
*With lush green boughs unchanging*
*Green when the summer sun is bright.*
*And when the forest's cold and white.*
*O Christmas Tree, O Christmas Tree,*
*With lush green boughs unchanging*

TRANSLATION OF "DER TANNENBAUM"
J. A. ZARNACK AND E. ANSHUTZ, 1820

very year, in a natural conifer woodland, a mass of tiny seedlings, self-sown, grow around the base of mature trees. Less that 1 per cent of them will survive to become forest giants, and then only if they have access to good light.

Before Christmas trees became so universally popular, the relatively few individuals mounting search parties for the perfect Christmas tree to dig up or cut from the local forests in Europe and North America would not have made much impact on conifer forest populations. Today, the best place to find a well-grown tree is at a Christmas-tree farm, garden centre or supermarket.

In the early 1900s the first tree farm was planted near Trenton, New Jersey by W.V. McGalliard. By the 1990s some 36 million Christmas trees were harvested annually in North America. In Britain, serious commercial production dates from the 1960s. Before that, trees were harvested from forestry thinnings. Now in the 1990s, around sixty growers account for about four million Christmas trees, with a further one million imported from Denmark and Belgium.

In Britain there are eight different pines, spruces or firs that are grown in large numbers to fulfil the seasonal demand. There are plans to introduce types popular in North America, such as balsam, Fraser and cork firs. In North America the

range of trees grown is much wider and there are a number of regional preferences, such as Douglas fir in the western states.

Common or Norway spruce (*Picea abies*), despite its tendency to drop its needles rather more quickly than other conifers, is still the most popular tree in Britain. The crème de la crème as far as needle-retention is concerned is the noble fir (*Abies procera*).

Scots pine (*Pinus sylvestris*) and Lodgepole pine (*Pinus contorta* var. *latifolia*), two similar species, both enjoyed in

Germany and North America because of their good needle-holding qualities, are becoming popular in Britain.

A great favourite with the Germans and Danes is the Nordmann or Caucasian fir (*Abies nordmanniana*). Its overall layered and uniform shape makes for a very stately tree with plenty of strong branches for ornaments and to hold candles steadily. However, in the 1990s sophisticated Christmas-tree shoppers, nostalgically searching for the tree that looks and smells like the one they had when they were children, complain that the Nordmann doesn't smell like a Christmas tree should. In Britain, the magazine *Gardening Which?* asked a sample of readers to "smell test" the Douglas Fir (*Pseudotsuga menziesii*), which some members of the British Christmas Tree Growers Association are now promoting. Widely grown and used throughout North America, it received approval for its lemon or pineapple fragrance from 75 per cent of those who took part in the survey.

Dubbed the designer tree, the Colorado blue spruce (*Picea pungens* 'Glauca'), with its silvery blue needles, has its own shimmery decorative look and makes a good foil for ornaments. It has fairly fierce needles, and so is best for the decor-conscious with children old enough to heed warnings not to touch the tree.

Just becoming popular in Britain, and already much used in North America, is the White, Colorado or Concolor fir (*Abies concolor*) with its soft needles and pale bluish green colour. If the magic of finding your own tree is too strong to ignore, there are many Christmas-tree farms in Europe and North America which offer their customers the option of digging up or cutting the tree of their choice. However, the majority of tree farmers harvest the trees themselves, to order, in successive waves from mid November through to 25 December, and

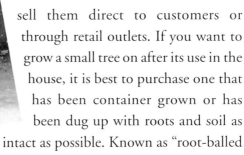

Christmas Greetings.

sell them direct to customers or through retail outlets. If you want to grow a small tree on after its use in the house, it is best to purchase one that has been container grown or has been dug up with roots and soil as intact as possible. Known as "root-balled and bagged" trees in Britain or "balled and burlapped" in North America, the root, soil and sacking must be kept damp until it can be potted into moist earth.

After Twelfth Night, or sooner for the tree's sake, shelter it in a cool shed for a few days to acclimatize it to harsher outdoors conditions. Then keep it watered and sheltered from strong winds. If you plan to use the same tree next year, use a larger pot and sink this into the ground. Next Christmas you can heave it out for another tour of indoor duty. But if you decide to let it loose in the garden, wait until spring before planting it in the ground. Then dig a hole large enough to take the tree's roots, add compost and plant the tree. Firm the surface soil, water well and apply a high nitrogen fertilizer to help the tree in its first year of freedom.

Growing your own tree from seed is a long haul, but one that might be fun for very patient children and parents. In autumn, soak seeds and pre-chill them according to seed packet instructions, then plant them into a tray of compost. Place the tray in a cold frame or unheated greenhouse. Keep the compost just moist and cover the seeds with a wire screen to protect them from mice. After three to four weeks the seeds will show signs of growth, with tiny leaves appearing at the soil surface. Water them regularly and, from spring onwards, be sure to keep the tray shaded.

After two or three years the seedlings will be 6-12in (15-30cm) tall and ready for transplanting. It will be some five years or more before your home-grown trees are big enough to bring indoors to decorate. Perhaps you won't have the heart to cut it down and will continue to enjoy it outdoors and buy cut trees from specialist growers for trimming!

The majority of trees used at Christmas are sold as cut trees. They have to be disposed of after the holiday season, and there are several ingenious suggestions from gardeners and recyclers of how to do this. The *Garbage Magazine* of Gloucester, Mass-achussetts, favours the ecological possibilities of using trees on beaches to rebuild eroded sand dunes.

Adding discarded Christmas trees to a bonfire is the least environmentally friendly method of getting rid of them but some communities in North America nevertheless make a great event out of their annual Twelfth Night fires. In several places in Indiana, all the discarded Christmas trees are gathered in one central location to be safely burned and the community enjoys the merrymaking.

In Britain many local authorities have arranged shredding schemes, where you can have your tree chipped and go away with it packed up in a bag to use as garden mulch.

Suggestions from North American recyclers include cutting the branches for kindling and collecting needles to add a pine scent to aromatic sachets.

Many gardeners suggest using the branches cut from large conifers as winter protection for garden plants. Some use the tree framework as a natural and inexpensive support for climbing plants to scramble up in summer.

Others add their trees to brush or wood piles in the garden, where they offer short-term habitats and cover for birds and other wildlife. Some even hang bird feeders from them, echoing, perhaps unknowingly, the Scandinavian custom of providing birds with a "tree" in winter. This Scandinavian offering to birds, dating from the seventeenth century, was in the shape of a wheatsheaf fixed in place at the top of a pole. Later adapted and decorated, it was called a Christmas pole.

The most ingenious idea of all comes from researchers at Ohio State University, who found that old trees weighted down with concrete and placed on lake or reservoir floors acted as havens for fish, increasing the catch rate of anglers!

Whatever tree you choose, and however you decide to recycle it, the moments you share with family and friends will outweigh the brief irritation of fallen needles as you enjoy the lustre of the tree, its pine fragrance and gleaming trimmings.

Research funded by growers in Europe and North America will no doubt eventually result in the perfect Christmas tree, bushy and pyramid-shaped, with numerous branches and no needle-fall until Twelfth Night!

White Fir – Abies concolor

# ￼REES FOR ALL

*With what shouts of joy we hailed the pretty Christmas Tree and with what glee and laughter we began to search amongst its twinkling lights and bright green leaves for the toys and sweetmeats that were hanging there, each one with a name written on its envelope.*

THE CHRISTMAS TREE
ANON, 1857

T̲he Christmas season is very much a time to share with the family, and the Christmas spirit of individual giving usually centres around the tree in the home. But there is also a strong tradition of outdoor or "public" trees, where communities come together to sing carols or perhaps even to auction the tree, to raise money for charity.

This custom of sharing a tree with others came about fairly early in the tree's modern history. A group of charitably minded ladies calling themselves The Dorcas Society of York, Philadelphia, advertised their tree-sharing event in 1830. Their advertisement invited visitors to an event they called a "Christmas tree", to view a decorated Christmas tree. The charge was six and a quarter cents per person.

In 1842, Charles Minnegerode, another German settled in Williamsburg, Virginia, shared his first Christmas tree in his new country with a neighbour, Judge Nathaniel Tucker. A contemporary report described how neighbours brought their children to see the tree, sing carols and take part in games. The tradition continued in the twentieth century when a community tree was set up every year near the former Tucker residence. In 1846 in Richmond, Virginia, a shopkeeper, August Bodeker, decorated a similar tree for friends and

neighbours in his shop. In the mid 1860s, it was quite customary to be asked to share a neighbour's tree and attend a "trimming party". At church, town hall or school "Christmas trees", there was usually a communal entertainment and gifts were hung from or placed under the tree. They were donations from parents or townsfolk and were chosen by lottery or labelled by the givers, so that everyone had a present.

At the turn of the century many cities and towns in North America began to put up trees in their squares or town centres.

In 1909 the first electrically lit, decorated public and outdoor tree was set up in Pasadena, California. It was followed quickly in 1910 by New York's first tree, a 60ft (18m) balsam fir in Madison Square Park. Boston also had its community tree on Boston Common. Philadelphia followed the next year.

Even though, by then, most homes in North America could boast a Christmas tree, the idea of public trees had taken firm hold and communities vied with each other to have the tallest, most dazzling tree. Seasonal journeys to see the Christmas lights, store decorations and public trees became part of the North American way of celebrating Christmas.

It also spread back to Europe and, around 1919, the use of decorated trees outdoors became popular in Germany, the original home of the Christmas tree.

After the First World War, community trees called "Trees of Light", symbolizing peace and goodwill were favoured by many North American towns and cities,with carols and patriotic hymns, as well as candle-light processions. Since the 1920s Living Christmas Tree Choirs have been a popular means of combining the secular and religious aspects of the season. Choristers climb into a huge tapering wooden frame,

covered by plastic tree greenery. They peek out, like large Christmas-tree ornaments, from each layer of greenery as they sing carols and hymns.

Trees themselves had become the gifts between one country and another, as well as between cities. Ever since 1947, London has had a tree in Trafalgar Square, given by the people of Norway in thanks for help during the Second World War. It is always a Norway spruce of sixty years or more, and measures about 70ft (21m) in height. After its arrival by sea, it is brought to Trafalgar Square by road and hoisted into place and deco-

rated with five hundred white lights, reminiscent of the candle-light favoured in Norwegian Christmas celebrations.

Boston, Massachussetts, has two such gift trees. The tree
that lights the city's Prudential Centre comes from the people
of the Canadian province of Nova Scotia, in thanks for the
assistance Bostonians gave them following a devastating explo-
sion in Halifax in 1917. The other tree, a 50ft (15m) spruce on
Boston Common, comes from New Brunswick, Canada, and
is a gift for the children of Boston. It marks Boston's help after
a tragic fire in 1877.

In North America public trees are just as important as individual trees in the home and the best known is probably the
one in New York's Rockefeller Center where there has been a
tree since 1931. In 1994, the 80ft (24m) Norway spruce, aged
about seventy, was a gift from a Connecticut couple who were
afraid it might fall on their house. More than 25,000 multi-
coloured bulbs strung on over five miles of wire illuminated
the tree and for the past forty years it has been topped by
the same 45in-wide (127.5cm) plastic star.

The tree is hoisted into place by a circus crane and
needs twenty people to set it up. In early December the
lights are switched on and the area around the Rockefeller Center comes to a standstill as New Yorkers and
visitors celebrate the official start to the Christmas season.

Of the many museums that greet the holiday season in this way, the Metropolitan Museum of Art, New York, is well known for its blue spruce decorated with eighteenth-century Neapolitan angels and cherubs. At its feet is a baroque nativity or crèche scene of two hundred Neapolitan figures, collected and donated by a museum benefactor, the late Mrs Loretta Howard.

Newest museum display of trees is that of the Florence Griswold Museum, at Old Lyme, Connecticut. Here thirty trees are dressed in nineteenth-century style to make the museum's Celebration of Holiday Trees. The Wadsworth Atheneum, Hartford, Connecticut, holds a Festival of Trees that collects over 12,000 toys for needy children in the state.

A similar fund-raising tree event in Britain revolved around trees designed and decorated by famous designer houses, including Gucci and Cartier. The lavishly ornamented trees were on display in one of London's city banks, before being auctioned on behalf of the Save the Children Fund.

In 1923 the American Forestry Association donated the first national tree to the White House. It was lit by President and Mrs Coolidge. In Washington today, presidential trees are an accepted part of the celebrations and in 1993 there were

reportedly at least twenty-one trees in various rooms, hallways and reception areas in the White House. The most publicized are those donated by members of the National Christmas Tree Association. Every year the Association, representing 2,100 growers, holds a competition, and each year two winners are chosen to provide the White House with trees for two consecutive years.

Adopting an attitude similar to that of their American counterparts, the British Christmas Tree Growers Association has, since 1982, made a gift of a tree for the decoration of Downing Street, the London home of the British Prime Minister.

Today the Christmas tree is everywhere, on ships, in shops, museums, palaces, town halls and hospitals, as well as in tiny cottages and grand houses. In 1994, even the *New York Times* adjusted its self-acknowledged "curmudgeonly" leader of 1883, when it announced in a lead editorial: "It is now our pleasant duty, 111 years after that first grumpy pronouncement, to declare officially that the Christmas tree is not a passing fad. Nor, if well watered, is it a lifeless corpse – at least not until the end of January."

A MERRY CHRISTMAS.
'Tis Christmas, with the snow and holly
So everyone is bright and jolly.

# Acknowledgements

With special thanks to: my parents for support and encouragement; Susan Conder for Christmas postcards; Pamela Egan, for information about Chrismons; Susan Lichten of New Haven, Connecticut and Hilda Morrill of Milton, Massachussetts for sending me newspaper cuttings; Gisela Mirwis for translations; Benjamin Perkins for his splendid illustrations of Christmas trees; Maurice Rickards and Elizabeth Greig for their unusual Christmas ephemera; Kay Sanecki for encouragement and information; Roy Vickery, editor of Plant-Lore for his notes on Christmas trees and Sally Williams of Garden Literature Press, Boston, for her dedicated searches through magazines, newspapers, libraries and bookstores for mentions of Christmas trees.

Thanks also to the following for providing me with relevant information: Embassy of the Federal Republic of Germany, London; Royal Norwegian Embassy, London; British Christmas Tree Growers Association; Christopher Hood of Yattendon Trees, Berkshire; Peter Jackson, Scotsdale Garden Centre, Cambridge, for information on tree nurseries; Elizabeth Kehoe of The Florence Griswold Museum, Old Lyme, Connecticut; Naomi Takafuchi, of the Metropolitan Museum of Art, New York; North Carolina Christmas Tree Association; Pacific Northwest Christmas Tree Assocation and Sandy Manly and Vince Silvestrie of the Rockefeller Center Press Office, New York. At Ebury Press, very many thanks to Cindy Richards and Alison Shackleton for making the book read so well and look so good.

The author and publisher would also like to thank the following photographers and organizations for their kind permission to reproduce the photographs in this book: Advertising Archives 57, 59; AKG London 16, 25, 31, 38, 48-9, 51, 75; Bridgeman Art Library: 3 (Private Collection), 12 (© Edmund Dulac, licensed by Hodder & Stoughton Limited), 13 (Private Collection), 14 (Royal Albert Memorial Museum, Exeter), 21-2 (Private Collection), 35-6 (Private Collection), 42 (Collection Kharbine, Paris), 43 (Victoria & Albert Museum, London), 45 (Victoria & Albert Museum, London), 50 (Private Collection), 55 (Worthing Museum & Art Gallery, Sussex), 63 (Private Collection), 76 (British Library, London); Dover Publications Inc 66 (above); Fine Art Photographic Library 1, 15, 19, 29, 44, 64 (Gavin Graham Gallery), 69, 79; Freies Deutsches Hochstift - Frankfurter Goethe-Museum 17; Impress Collection 11, 28, 33, 37, 62, 65, 66 (below right), 67, 72; Jean-Loup Charmet 18, 23-4, 56, 58 (right), 73, 78; Mary Evans Picture Library 2, 7, 30, 32, 74; Maurice Rickards Collection 10, 20, 34, 39, 46-7, 54, 58 (top left), 64 (insert), 68.

Every effort has been made to contact all the copyright owners of the quotations used in this book, but in some cases this has not been possible and we apologize for any inconvenience this may cause.

# Select Bibliography

Baker, Margaret, *Discovering Christmas Customs & Folklore*, Princes Risborough, Bucks; Shire Publications, 1992: Brenner, Robert, *Christmas Past*, Westchester Pennsylvania; Schiffer, 1986: Brimble, L. J.F., *Trees in Britain*, London; Macmillan 1948: Foley, Daniel, *The Christmas Tree*, Philadelphia; Chiltern Company, 1961: Hedley, Olwen, *Queen Charlotte*, London; John Murray, 1975: Miles, Clement A., *Christmas Customs and Traditions, Their History and Significance,* New York; Dover, 1976: Miller, Daniel, *Unwrapping Christmas*, Oxford; Clarendon Press, 1993: Snyder, Phillip, *The Christmas Tree Book*, New York; Viking Press, 1976: Tille, A., *Yule & Christmas*, London; David Nutt, 1899: Weber-Kellermann, Ingeborg, *Das Weinachtsfest*, Luzern and Frankfurt; C. T. Bucher, 1978.